E. G. DAWSON

How to Master Your Finances

A Simple Guide to Easy Budgeting

First edition

This book was professionally typeset on Reedsy. Find out more at reedsy.com

Happiness is not in the mere possession of money; it lies in the joy of achievement, in the thrill of creative effort.

FRANKLIN D. ROOSEVELT

Contents

1

Introduction

Welcome to the ultimate financial roller coaster, where budgeting is not just about numbers—it's the VIP pass to the coolest concert of your life: Your Money Symphony! Think of budgeting as your personal financial DJ, making sure every dollar dances to the right beat.

There are so many resources out there for people to be able to create their own budget. But I wanted a book that was simple and straightforward. Where the essential information is all in one place and gives you a step by step guide on the basics of creating a budget.

So, why should you care about this budgeting stuff? Well, imagine your money is like a pizza (who doesn't love a good pizza, am I right?). Budgeting is the secret sauce that ensures each slice goes exactly where it's meant to—no rogue pepperonis causing chaos! Financial success isn't just for the number-savvy suits, it is for anyone passionate about their money and wanting to pave the way towards their financial independence. It's as simple as that. Gear up, and embrace the journey, and know that every effort you put into mastering your budget is a step closer to financial triumph.

We all know how thrilling, and scary, adulting can be. Our goal is to alleviate some of that fear when it comes to our finances. In a world full of economic uncertainties, budgeting is your superhero cape. It's the Robin to your Batman, the Chewbacca to your Han Solo, the Goose to your Maverick, the... Well, you get the point. This book isn't here to bore you with endless spreadsheets. We're on a mission to make budgeting easy and understandable for anyone new to the process. A budget is your secret weapon. It's the master plan that turns financial worries into mere speed bumps on your road to prosperity. We will wade through these challenges together. Forget the confusion and frustration - we're here to sprinkle some budgeting fairy dust and make your financial journey as clear as a blue sky.

My budgeting journey started in 2019 after some personal hardships had been thrust upon me that took my life in a completely different direction than I had always imagined it would. Not having a choice to go it alone but found the courage to move forward anyway, I found something I could focus my energy on. I am sure you can join me in saying that this is just a part of life. And it is the crappy part of life, isn't it? But it is how you handle these challenges that really molds a person into who they are. You have to see some of these setbacks as opportunities for growth. I've come to understand that the essence of resilience lies not in avoiding hardships but in navigating them with grace, emerging on the other side with newfound wisdom. Do I believe I am a wise person? Absolutely not. I still have a long road to travel on that path but it is the perspective that I gain through each challenge that I will never take for granted. So, I didn't have time to sit around and say, "poor me." Well, truth be told, I may have carved out some time to feel sorry for myself but it really didn't do me any favors to dwell. I had a family to take care of so I had to pull myself together and I started by taking control of my finances. One step at a time. You can do it too - and you are not alone on this adventure.

2

Setting Clear Financial Goals

The best way to stay on track with your budgeting journey is to set clear goals. Just like anything else in life, the probability of succeeding increases tremendously if you have goals for yourself. Short-term financial goals are stepping stones toward long term financial success, providing tangible and achievable targets to enhance financial stability and flexibility. They help guide your focus in a clear direction so you know to concentrate your time, energy, and resources in what truly matters. In this case, your financial well-being. Having defined goals sparks motivation. They serve as the fuel to propel you forward, turning aspirations into accomplishments. These are your decision making anchors. They assist in making choices aligned with your objectives, preventing distractions or detours that may lead you off course. By setting goals, you hold yourself accountable for your actions. This accountability cultivates discipline and a sense of responsibility crucial for personal and professional growth. Achieving goals, even small ones, boosts confidence. Each success, no matter how incremental they may be, contributes to a positive self-perception and encourages you to tackle more significant challenges.

I want you to think about some goals you may have already been playing around with. Separate them into short term goals and long term goals. Maybe you have some smaller home maintenance projects you have been meaning to complete. Or maybe you don't even own a home but your dream is to purchase your own one day. Is there a vacation you have been wanting to go on? What about a new computer or phone you have been patiently waiting for the right time to upgrade? Whatever your goal may be, write it down on paper so you have a clear understanding of what it will cost to get there. I will advise you to prioritize your goals based on urgency and importance. If you are in need of living space, I suggest finding a suitable place to live would come before purchasing a new computer. So be smart about your goals.

When writing these down, I want you to think about the achievability of these goals. Are they attainable? Be realistic about setting short term goals. Setting these goals is like giving your financial journey a turbo boost. They provide clear milestones that keep you motivated and focused. These goals act as building blocks, creating a sense of accomplishment and propelling you toward your larger financial aspirations. Think of these short term goals as the GPS guiding you through the twists and turns of your financial path, ensuring you stay on track and celebrate victories along the way. Trust me, once you start hitting these milestones, you will feel empowered. You will have the confidence and proof to know that you can do it.

Now that you have your financial goals listed out and priori-
tized, set these aside for now and let's move on. We will come
back to these later.

3

Understanding Your Financial Situation

One thing I want you all to understand is it doesn't matter what your income is, you can still budget and set a goal with your money. Whether you are making $1,000 a month, or $10,000 a month, your goal is still the same. Obviously, if you are making that much a month then you can get to your goals quicker, but that is not the point. The point is to be in charge of your money and know exactly what is coming in and going out. It is not a race, or a competition. This is just you and your money.

First things first, let's talk about income -the superhero paycheck that swoops in to save the day. Identify your income sources. Salary? Check. Side Hustle? Even better. Now onto expenses - these can be sneaky. Aside from your normal bills i.e. rent, utilities, groceries, gas, you've got to nail down all those recurring expenses that add up on a regular basis. Do you get your hair and nails done? Don't forget to include your daily trips to the coffee shop. And what about those automated payments to your free-trial sign ups you've collected and forgotten about along the way? TV subscriptions? Definitely. Dating apps? Guilty. Hey, I've been there too so I can't blame you on that one. You wouldn't believe the people that don't have a clue what subscriptions they signed up for or what they are paying because they do not keep a budget or even look at their bank account on a regular basis. Or maybe you can believe it, because you are guilty in at least some part of that statement. Need not fear, you're on the right path to take back control of your finances.

What I want you to do now, is grab a piece of paper and write down your sources of income on the left side and your expenses, all listed out, on the right side. It does not have to be pretty. We are just rough drafting it to get an idea. Keep in mind this would be everything for the entire month. You may get paid bi-weekly but we will talk about that more in depth later. Now total up each column. I would hope you are left with a positive balance. This is where we need to be real with ourselves. We need to look at the expenses column and prioritize it. What is a necessity? What is a non-negotiable must-have that you enjoy doing that you just can't get rid of? What are the expenses you are paying for but never use? Are there any other cheaper options or versions you can manage to get by on if you feel it is necessary? You need to ask these questions to yourself and answer them honestly. Once you have a general idea, then we can move on. Even better if you crossed off one or two expenses that you feel you do not need. Your list should look a little something like this:

Income:
  Salary $4,000

Expenses:
  Rent $1,800
  Utilities $80 Left Over $780
  Groceries $400
  Gas $200
  Insurance $100
  Phone $100
  Cable/TV $40
  Car Payment $500

Income $4,000 - Expenses $3,220 = **$780 Left Over**

With this mock budget, you can see there is $780 left over after your necessary expenses. This would be money left that you pay for the unexpected expenses that arise. Birthdays, doctor appointments, eating out, etc.

Serious question, before writing down your income and expenses, did you know how much money you had left over after your necessary expenses? How about how much money is left overall after the unexpected expenses? Did you realize how much you were spending on unexpected expenses? Sometimes we don't realize how much we're spending unless we can see it in front of us and track it, such as on a budget sheet.

4

Creating a Realistic Budget

When you first sit down to create your budget, it can be a little overwhelming. This is why we are taking it one step at a time. Once you have your initial budget set, proactively keeping your budget updated will not take very much time at all. So hang in there, we are getting closer.

There are many different styles of budgeting that you can use to help stay on track. I am only going to talk about a few. Each method will have its pros and cons so you need to pick the one that works best for you. Something that is easily understood and can be updated on a regular basis. You don't have to just choose one option either. Play around with it and combine different methods, if needed, for you to use in a way you're comfortable with.

One popular method, and one I like to use, is the zero-based budgeting method. This means that your income minus your expenses equals zero. The purpose of zero based budgeting is to allocate all of your funds to something so you don't willingly just spend, spend, spend. You know what is allocated, that way you can stay on track with your money. So what about that $780 that was left over with that mock budget we did? How do you get to zero dollars? Well, you create categories for those unexpected expenses. Because if we're being honest, they are not entirely unexpected, are they? We decide and plan to eat out, we schedule doctor appointments, and correct me if I am wrong, but birthdays come along the same time every year, right? Think about the current month you are in. Any birthdays that you intend to buy gifts for? Any holidays you need to allocate extra money towards? Each month's budget will look slightly different depending on what you have going on, and that is okay. As long as you have your money allocated then you should have a sense of relief knowing that you have a plan for where your money is going and it is not a surprise. Another category, or allocation, to think about would be eating out. Set a certain amount of money aside each month for dining out. Be reasonable. If you know you were spending way too much on Taco Bell, then cut it back. Don't forget about a savings allocation. This is very important to be able to reach your short term goals you set forth in the beginning of this journey. So remember to set aside a certain amount towards your savings goals. This is your budget and your money, so have fun with it.

Another main method of budgeting is the 50/30/20 rule. Basically, 50% of your income goes to your necessary expenses, 30% goes to your unnecessary expenses, and 20% goes towards savings. If you are a number person, then maybe this is the method for you. Or if you have a set salary and you have the same amount of money coming in each month. This is different from the zero based method because you allocate percentage amounts versus dollar amounts. This is a more recent system used by many so if this method makes sense to you, then run with it.

A third budgeting method, and one that has become very popular, is the envelope method. This may be for you if you just can't get a control on your spending. If running a plastic card is too easy for you or if you find yourself lacking the discipline to stay on budget, then this could be your standard method. At least to get you on track to change your ways. In this method, you would divide your cash into envelopes marked for different spending categories. Once an envelope is empty, you're done spending in that category for the month. You could have an envelope each for groceries, eating out, fun, clothing, misc spending, etc. This will ensure that you do not overspend in certain categories.

Do you get paid once a month, or bi-weekly? This can be used to your advantage also. You can align your budget with your bi-weekly pay schedule, ensuring you allocate funds and expenses as evenly as possible for each pay period. This can help in managing your money more effectively. Pay attention to when your automatic payments or monthly bills come out of your account and adjust them, if possible, so you have an even amount of outgoing versus incoming. You don't want your budget to be lopsided. That can lead to frustration on one pay period as you may have plenty of money left after one paycheck, but hardly anything after the other.

5

Tools and Resources for Budgeting

These days, we have so many options literally at our fingertips. If you search for budgeting apps on your phone right now, there will be plenty that come up. You don't need a fancy-shmancy app to track your spending, just one that does the basics. If you find an app that you feel is right and easy for you to use, then stick with that. This way it will be with you whenever and wherever. You're meant to be together, just like Shakira says.

There is also the good ole Excel spreadsheet. If you are OCD like me, then this is a good way to stay in control of, well everything. Track it down to the penny. Yes, that is my OCD talking. You don't actually have to track it to the last penny, but if you can, why not? It doesn't have to be Excel. It can be Google Sheets if that fits better with your comfort level. The benefit of using a blank sheet is you can make it look however you want it to.

Certain websites offer educational resources, articles, and budgeting guides to enhance financial literacy and empower informed decision making. Along with other books and blogs with success stories that can inspire and guide you throughout your journey. Or if you are not a big reader and don't want to put more time into reading, you can listen to numerous podcasts about budgeting and financial knowledge that can help you along the way.

Say you are succeeding at this budgeting thing. You think, this is pretty darn easy and feels great to know where my money is going. Then, you see a sale on those expensive sunglasses you really wanted and you tell yourself, "I should be rewarded for doing so well on my budget." So you spend a few hundred dollars on those sick sunglasses. Then you see something else, and you start to justify that purchase and then it just snowballs. It is easy to go back to our old ways. To get back on track, it is good to routinely commit yourself to spending challenges, or spending freezes. A spending freeze is where you challenge yourself to strictly limit discretionary expenses for a period of time. It could be for a few weeks or a few months. It's a fun way to reset spending habits and boost savings. Be disciplined and smart with your money.

Now that you have researched some different methods and looked up various budgeting apps, I want you to take that scratch paper you created with your initial budget and take the time to create a realistic budget using the method and source of your choice. This does not have to be perfect, just get the information in there as a starting point but try and be as precise as you can. This will allow you to see the areas you need adjustments in. Whether it be how much you spend in certain miscellaneous categories or how much you can put towards your debts or towards your savings.

6

Debt and Saving

This wouldn't be a book about financial success if we didn't talk about debt. It is such an ugly word and in today's world, it is common and encouraged to carry debt. This is the most backwards way of thinking.

For one, debt comes with the unwelcome companion of interest. The average interest rate on a credit card today is nearly 28%. That is mind blowing to me. The longer you carry debt, the more interest accrues. And at 28%, yikes! No wonder our nation has a debt issue. This can turn a small financial hiccup into a full blown headache and that would only be for one credit card. More than likely, the average person has two to four credit cards at a time. That is a lot of interest accrued. You can say that you are one of those disciplined people that pay off your credit card in full each month so that it doesn't accrue interest and you get the benefits of whatever rewards the credit card company is offering. But I hardly believe that you are that type of person if you are reading this book. Trust me, I believed I was that type of person. After I was a couple of years into my obsessive budgeting, I thought I was responsible enough to have a credit card again. Turns out I was wrong. We learn these things about ourselves while we are on this journey so that is why it is important to be realistic about not just our skills, but also our faults. It would be ideal to be able to learn from other people's mistakes. It would save us a lot of time. Unfortunately, that is not really how life works, is it? We usually end up having to learn hard lessons from our own mistakes. Hopefully we can try and eliminate some of those mistakes by gaining knowledge from others that can help us on this journey.

Secondly, if you are juggling multiple credit cards, then your budget is juggling multiple credit card payments. Constantly juggling debt payments can take a toll on your mental well-being. The stress of meeting deadlines and the looming burden of debt can lead to anxiety and sleepless nights. Do yourself a favor, pick one debt and focus on paying it off. Then move to another and do the same. Start with the lowest amount owed. Or start with the one that has the highest interest rate. Whether it's a credit card or school loan, it doesn't really matter. Whichever makes sense to you, just do it. And don't give up because it can be done. I know you can do it, you just have to have the discipline and willpower to stay focused on the task at hand.

Society makes us believe that debt is a normal way of life. To be able to have a good credit score to buy a house, or a car. But in reality, it's a vicious debt circle that goes round and round. Do some people believe that you can purchase a car outright? Heck yes. Some even believe you can purchase a house outright. To some, that might seem impossible, but know that it is doable.

If that is one of your long term goals, then go for it. Don't let anyone stop you, or tell you what you can or can't do with your money. Remember this is your money, your budget, and your journey.

I could go on and on about debt but I want to keep it simple. Pay it off. If you have wracked up a lot of debt, your short term goals should be first the debts you owe. They should come before any other goals that you have. Credit cards, student loans, car payments, set a goal and pay them off. One by one. This is important in starting your journey to financial success. You can't build wealth if you owe a ton of money. Don't be discouraged. I know looking down that list of credit you've borrowed can feel like a set back. Time to be an adult and do the hard things so you can succeed. It's possible. I know it. You know it. Don't have much or any debt? Way to go! You've just skipped a step and are that much closer to your objective.

Once your debt is paid off, then you can move your focus onto saving. Saving is a very important part of budgeting. What do you have to show for your hard work if you have nothing in the bank? Life is unpredictable. Having savings provides a financial safety net to navigate unexpected expenses, whether it's a medical emergency, sudden job loss, car or home repairs. Wouldn't it be awesome if you were able to cover these unexpected emergencies with actual money, rather than credit? This would be called, wait for it, an emergency fund. Yes, adulting can be rough sometimes but it can also be rewarding when you are in a financial state where you can cover emergency expenses on your own, without relying on anyone else or any plastic assistance. Having a financial reserve provides a sense of security which can reduce stress and anxiety associated with financial instability. It brings peace of mind and allows you to focus on your goals and aspirations without the constant worry of living paycheck to paycheck.

To be financially independent and know that you are capable of taking care of yourself and your family, well that is truly an empowering thought. And if that is not motivation enough, then I don't know what is.

7

Overcoming Common Budget Pitfalls

One of the biggest reasons people don't want to start a budget is because they think it is too complex and that they don't have time. The misconception that budgeting requires advanced financial knowledge can scare someone into taking the first step. You do not need prior financial knowledge to keep and track a budget. Literally anyone can do it. Trust me, the longest and hardest part is getting started only because you have to finally stop avoiding the fact that maybe you are not handling your money as well as you know you should be. And sometimes that realization is scary. Once you have your initial budget created, all you need to do is spend five to ten minutes each week checking your budget. Time is not an excuse. We all have twenty four hours in a day, it's just how we prioritize and use that time.

Set realistic goals. Setting overly ambitious goals without meeting smaller milestones along the way can lead to frustration and failure. Along with drastically cutting your expenses. Pick one or two items you don't really need or can live without and cut those. The further along you get in your budgeting journey, the more experience and knowledge you'll gain and you can continue to cut unnecessary expenses out over time.

Be flexible. No matter which method you choose, allow yourself to be able to modify and change it where necessary. If something comes up, you want to be flexible with your budget so you don't end up over spending. You don't want to be stressed out either, so leaving a little extra for flexibility can benefit not just your budget, but your mental well being.

Failure to allocate funds for emergencies can derail a budget. Without a safety net, sudden financial challenges can lead to budgeting setbacks. Start with a goal of $1,000 as a safety net. Then grow it. Grow it to where if there was a sudden emergency, you would have enough to cover it. And don't stress about using it for that reason. That is why it is there.

Succumbing to the allure of impulse purchases without considering the budget can undermine financial plans. Impulse spending can sabotage efforts to save or stick to spending limits. This is easy to do when you see your social media page where your friends are off vacationing to beautiful places. It is so tempting to give in. But don't, not just yet. You have to reach your goals first. That is why you set them. Be clear with your friends and family about your financial goals. If they are asking you to go out a lot and do things, you will need to stand up and not be afraid to say, "Sorry guys, not tonight. It is not in my budget."

If you and your spouse are going through this journey together, then communication is the key to success. That is what they say, is it not? Within your marriage as well. Communication is everything. Poor communication, misalignment of financial goals and lack of cooperation can all impede budgeting efforts. You don't always have to agree, but you will have to compromise. I am sure you have heard that many times before. The most common thing you will see is that one spouse will be in it all the way and the other will have just one foot in the door. And that is okay too. As long as you meet together once a week, or even once every two weeks, heck maybe it's once a month, for five to ten minutes to go over the important points of your budget, then you are succeeding.

Stay motivated. Do what you have to do to keep yourself moving through those milestones and reaching your goals. Put sticky notes on your mirror. Create a vision board. Tell a friend, or better yet, have the friend work through this journey alongside you. Keep each other accountable on your regular budget checks and spending habits. Do whatever it takes. Don't stop because you made a bad decision or something really unexpected came up. These are just speed bumps. Get back at it, stay with it. You will never get anywhere if you don't get up and try again. And again. And again.

8

Tracking and Adjusting your Budget

Major life events such as a job change, marriage, or having children can impact your budget. You will need to adjust your budget accordingly to accommodate new priorities and responsibilities.

Periodically reassess your financial goals. Adjust them based on changes in income, expenses, or personal circumstances. Align your budget with these updated goals to ensure they remain achievable. You should also be regularly reviewing your expenses as time goes on and you get more comfortable with your budgeting skills.Identify areas where you can cut back. Eliminating unnecessary spending frees up funds that can be redirected towards savings or essential needs, such as an increased grocery budget for your growing family.

If you have a fluctuating income, plan for both high and low-income scenarios. This helps ensure your budget remains realistic and sustainable, even during periods of income variability. An example of this would be if you work on commission. You could have an incredibly profitable month and then turn around and be scraping by the next. The point in preparing for income variability is so you wouldn't have to be scraping by.

Re-evaluate your emergency fund based on changes in your personal circumstances. Maybe you have had your emergency fund at a certain amount when you started your budget five years ago. Think about what has changed since then and what new financial emergencies are possible in your current lifestyle and adjust accordingly.

Don't forget irregular or annual expenses like insurance premiums or holiday spending. Set aside a portion of your budget and make an allocation, or envelope, for these specific occasional expenses to avoid surprises. We all know the impending fear of Christmas spending. Set a max budget you intend to spend for Christmas and divide it by twelve. Then set aside that amount each month, all year long, to help save for it so you can go into the holiday season knowing you can avoid the stress that usually comes with it and you get to enjoy the reasons for the season.

9

Conclusion

Look back at your goals you wrote out at the beginning of this book. After creating a sensible budget, are the goals you wrote also sensible? If not, adjust them. Do you have debt? You may need to prioritize your goals if you have debt owed.

Which budgeting method did you choose to start with? Did you include all your income and expenses? Were you able to whittle down some unnecessary expenses to make it more manageable and flexible? Your successful budgeting is a testament to your dedication, adaptability, and the belief that financial freedom is not a distant dream but a tangible reality within your grasp.

What source did you use to keep your budget in one place? Apps are very handy as you can make adjustments whenever you need to. Or a simple excel spreadsheet that you have access to daily or weekly. Whatever it may be, it needs to be easily accessible and reliable for you to make tweaks along the way.

Take a good look at what you have just achieved and take a moment to revel in your triumphs. Your budget, once a mere scribble on paper, has transformed into a powerful tool to guide you through these challenges. Were you skeptical at first? You have done the hard part, my friend. Now, what you have before you is a roadmap to your success. A budget that you are in control of. It is not just about the dollars and cents; it's about the newfound confidence, the peace of mind, that comes with mastering your financial narrative. Remember that budgeting is not a one time event but a lifelong adventure. Embrace it with curiosity, resilience, and the knowledge that you have the power to reach your financial goals and conquer the world. Okay, maybe not conquer the world, but you get the point. So many possibilities lie ahead. Good luck on your financial journey. I wish you all the best. I believe you can do it. And by now, I hope you believe in yourself as well.

If you found this book to be helpful, I would be extremely grateful if you could take just 60 seconds to kindly leave an honest review of the book on Amazon. Please share your feedback and thoughts for others to see.

10

Resources

Black, M. (2024, January 22). What is the average credit card interest rate this week? January 22, 2024. Forbes Advisor. https://www.forbes.com/advisor/credit-cards/average-credit-card-interest-rate/

Cruze, R. (2023, August 29). How to budget with the cash envelope system. Ramsey Solutions. https://www.ramseysolutions.com/budgeting/envelope-system-explained

Kagan, J. (2023, April 23). Zero-Based Budgeting: What it is and how to use it. Investopedia. https://www.investopedia.com/terms/z/zbb.asp

Pokora, B. (2023, March 9). Credit card Statistics and Trends 2024. Forbes Advisor. https://www.forbes.com/advisor/credit-cards/credit-card-statistics/

Smith, K. A. (2023, June 14). What is the 50/30/20 rule? Forbes Advisor. https://www.forbes.com/advisor/banking/guide-to-50-30-20-budget/

OpenAI. (2024). ChatGPT 3.5. Retrieved from https://www.openai.com/